AN ANCHOR
for the
SOUL

AN ANCHOR
for the
SOUL

BIBLE STUDY

RAY PRITCHARD

MOODY PRESS
CHICAGO

Table of Contents

Introduction

This Bible study was written for people who want to know God. If that describes you, then I have some good news for you. It is possible for you to know God deeply and personally, and, by knowing God, you can experience His power in your life. This good news doesn't come from me. It comes from God Himself. In the Bible this good news is called the "gospel." The gospel is good news because it tells what God has done so that men and women can come into a personal relationship with the One who made them.

Let me say right up front that this Bible study will be helpful no matter where you might be on your spiritual journey. When it comes to knowing God, we all stand in different places. Some are seekers, some are doubters, some are skeptics, and some know very little about the Christian faith. Others were raised in a church but drifted away years ago. If you would like to know God, that's all that matters. You may count yourself as a religious person or you may think of yourself as non-religious. That's fine either way. Many people today have a deep interest in spiritual matters even though they are not part of any religious organization. My goal is not to convince you to join a particular church, but to help you find a personal relationship with Jesus Christ.

I'm sure you have a few questions. I hope so, because honest questions deserve good answers. Here are some questions you may have:

> *What is God like?*
> *How can I know Him?*
> *Am I really a sinner?*
> *How can my sins be forgiven?*
> *Who is Jesus and what did He do?*
> *What must I do to be saved?*
> *What does it mean to be a Christian?*
> *How can I find peace with God?*
> *How can I be sure I am going to heaven?*

The story of the Bible is Good News that can change your life. It tells us about ourselves, our deepest problems, and God's amazing solution to those problems. More than that, it presents to us the person of Jesus Christ and describes the new life He offers to one and all. This is the supreme message of the Bible. Even if you have doubts or questions about the Bible, I encourage you to complete this Bible study with an open mind and then decide for yourself what you believe.

If you haven't yet read *An Anchor for the Soul* (Moody Press, 2000), I highly recommend that you do so. Although this Bible study is designed as a stand-alone guide, you'll gain much more if you use the Bible study and the book together. The Bible study builds on the book by using a variety of tools to help you go deeper, especially in the area of personal application.

You'll also find it helpful to have a modern translation of the Bible, such as the English Standard Version, the New American Standard Bible, or the New International Version, as you go through these lessons. There are a number of good study Bibles that will give you extensive notes on the biblical text. I recommend the Ryrie Study Bible, the MacArthur Study Bible, the Nelson Study Bible, and the NIV Study Bible. You also might want to consider having a Bible dictionary handy, along with a concordance to help you find key verses in the Bible.

The eight sessions in this Bible study can be used in a small-group discussion, a Sunday school class, or in one-on-one discipleship. However, the material is written so that it is just as effective for individual study.

Before we begin, here's a simple tip. Don't rush through these sessions. You'll gain much more if you take time to think about the questions and write out your answers. You'll also find great value in looking up the various Bible verses one by one. As you go through the Anchor Bible study, ask God to open your heart to His truth. Your attitude will determine how much you get out of this study. God invites us to seek Him with a whole heart. As you respond to what you learn, the Holy Spirit will be at work in you, enlightening your mind, opening your heart, and shaping you into the image of Jesus Christ. So don't be surprised if you end up a different person when you are finished. That's my prayer as you journey through these eight Bible study sessions.

BEFORE YOU BEGIN . . .

—◦ *What questions would you like answered during this Bible study?*

—◦ *Where do you hope to be on your spiritual journey when you have finished the Anchor Bible study?*

— SESSION ONE —
A Place to Begin

PART ONE —
STARTING THE JOURNEY

We were made to know God and something in us desperately wants to know Him. We are incurably religious by nature. That's why every human society—no matter how primitive—has some concept of a higher power, some vision of a reality that goes beyond the natural. On one level that explains why science has not eradicated religion from the earth. Science can never do that because technological achievement can't meet the deepest needs of the human heart. That explains why millions of people read their horoscopes every morning and millions more watch or call psychic hotlines.

We want to know the answers to the three most basic questions of life: Where did I come from? Why am I here? Where am I going? And we will spend money, buy books, listen to tapes, attend seminars, and travel great distances to find the answers. It is the same everywhere on earth. Superficially we are very different in our appearance, background, language, and customs. But scratch deeper and you discover that all people are substantially the same. Once past the surface, you discover no fundamental difference between a person born in poverty in Haiti and a corporate lawyer on Wall Street, or between a schoolteacher in Ethiopia and a computer scientist in Singapore. Everywhere we are the same—with the same longings, regrets, dreams, and hopes, the same need to love and be loved, the same desire to be remembered after we die, and with the same sense that there must be a God of some kind who made us.

We were made to know God and we need to know Him. God made us to know Him. He designed us so that we would want to know Him—and then He guaranteed we wouldn't be happy unless He Himself fills the void within. This brings us face-to-face with the famous statement that there is a "God-shaped vacuum" inside each person. We may turn to God or we may fill the vacuum with idols of our own making or the evil spirits of our ancestors. Something in us drives us to seek ultimate meaning outside ourselves. That "something" inside us is put there by God. Augustine gave us this oft-quoted prayer: "You have made us for yourself, and our hearts are restless until they find their rest in you."

But who is God and what is He like? We need to know the answer to that question before we can come to know Him personally. In this session, we're going to let the Bible tell us about our Heavenly Father. As we do so, ask the Lord to give you a heart open to His truth.

—◦ *Which of the following best describes where you are on your spiritual journey right now?*

❑ Seeker

❑ Honest Doubter

❑ Frustrated Skeptic

❑ True Believer

❑ Casual Onlooker

❑ Spiritual but Not Religious

❑ Former Believer

❑ Mostly Confused

❑ Hopelessly Lost

> Everything in this Bible study is based on one central truth: You were made to know God and you can't and won't be truly satisfied until you know Him.
> Nothing this world offers can take the place of knowing God.
>
> Do you agree that you were made to know God? Would you like to know God better? Why or why not?

—◦ *If you could ask God one question about your relationship with Him, what would it be?*

_____

_____

_____

—◦ *Are you seeking to know God better? If so, the good news is that God welcomes all those who truly seek Him. What do the following verses tell us the importance of seeking God?*

Deuteronomy 4:29

_____

_____

_____

Jeremiah 29:11

_____

_____

Matthew 7:7–8

_____

_____

_____

_____

Hebrews 11:6

_____

_____

_____

_____

PART TWO ⌒
WHO IS GOD?

A ONE-MINUTE QUIZ

In the space below, write out your personal definition of God in twenty words or less, taking no more than one minute to do it.

⌒ *Why is it important that we have a correct view of God? What happens when our view of God is somehow distorted?*

⌒ *According to Psalm 19:1–6, what can we learn about God by studying the skies?*

—∘ *What do these Old Testament passages tell us about who God is?*

Exodus 34:5–7 _____

Psalm 103:8–13 _____

Isaiah 6:1–3 _____

Isaiah 40:21–26 _____

Daniel 4:34–37 _____

—∘ *Read Nehemiah 1. How did Nehemiah's knowledge of God give him courage to pray boldly when faced with a difficult challenge?*

—∘ *Which is harder for you to believe—that God loves you and wants a relationship with you, or that God will someday judge you because of your sins?*

_____

_____

_____

SIX FACTS ABOUT GOD

1 He eternally exists in Three Persons (Matthew 28:19–20).

2 He is the Sovereign Lord (Psalm 115:3).

3 He created all things (Hebrews 11:3).

4 He made you in His image (Genesis 1:26–27).

5 He knows all about you (Psalm 139:1–4).

6 He cares about you (Jeremiah 29:11).

PART THREE ∘—
THE MAN WHO HAD IT ALL
(Ecclesiastes 1–2)

Ecclesiastes is one of the most fascinating and misunderstood books of the Bible. It is a book written by a man of faith (Solomon probably) who leads his readers on a voyage through some of the backwater regions of life that we all think about but don't discuss in public. He isn't afraid to ask the hard questions and to admit when there are no easy answers. You might call it a kind of Old Testament apologetic in which the author invites his readers to join him on a search for ultimate truth.

—○ *How would you classify the book? Is it . . .*

Fatalistic—7:13–14	**Pessimistic**—4:2–3	**Materialistic**—3:19–21
Hedonistic—3:12–13	**Hopeless**—1:9–11	**Heretical**—7:16–17

Chew the cud on this one: *Does the Bible present a view of life that is basically pessimistic or basically optimistic?* (Name your own option if you don't like the first two choices.)

—○ *As Solomon searched for the meaning of life, he tried many possibilities. Describe what he found in each area.*

A Wisdom 1:12–18 _____

B Mirth and Pleasure 2:1–3 _____

C Earthly Possessions 2:4–9 _____

D Unlimited Indulgence 2:10 _____

—○ *What conclusion does he come to in 2:11? Why does he say, "I hated life" in 2:17?*

GRASPING AT SHADOWS

When the final examination grades at Cambridge University were published, Henry Martyn's highest ambition had been realized. He was the honors man of the year. Strangely, his first sensation was keen disappointment. "I obtained my highest wishes," he said, "but was surprised that I had grasped a shadow." Why is it that our dreams when finally realized and our goals when finally achieved often bring less satisfaction than we had hoped—and often bring a sense of disappointment? What does this teach us about life and about God?

PART FOUR ⌒
LOOKING IN ALL THE WRONG PLACES

This picture illustrates the human predicament. Although we desperately want to know God, our sins have separated us from Him. Nothing we do can bridge the gap.

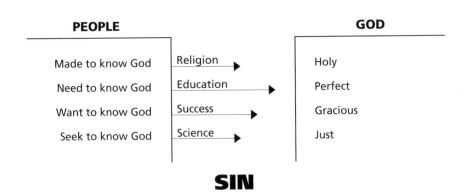

- Name some other ways people try to find God and true meaning and purpose in life:

- Why is it that none of our "bridges" make it all the way from where we are to where God is? If our "bridges" won't cross the SIN chasm, who must build the bridge for us?

BEFORE WE WRAP UP . . .

Have you discovered what life is all about? Life is nothing without God. Everything else is just details. Knowing the God who made you is the most important thing in life. It gives meaning and purpose to everything else. If you don't know God, nothing else matters. If you live for eighty years but don't discover that truth, you've missed the very reason for your own existence. If you should earn a million dollars—or ten million dollars—and have hundreds of friends and the praise of your contemporaries, if you have all that but don't figure out this basic truth, you're still in spiritual kindergarten. So the question we need to ask is this: Do you know God, and if you don't, would you like to know Him?

A VERSE TO MEMORIZE

"And this is eternal life, that they know you the only true God, and Jesus Christ whom you have sent."

—⌕ John 17:3 ESV

A PRAYER FOR SEEKERS OF SPIRITUAL TRUTH

f this prayer expresses the desire of your heart, put your initials next to it.

O God, I want to know You. If You are really there, please reveal Yourself to me. Show me the truth about myself. Open my eyes and create faith in my heart. Give me the gift of an open mind to receive Your truth. Help me to come to know You. Grant that my deepest questions may be answered with Your truth. Help me to seek You with all my heart. And may I find You and be satisfied with what I find. Amen.

A Truth to Remember

IF YOU LIVE FOR EIGHTY YEARS
BUT DON'T KNOW THE GOD
WHO CREATED YOU, YOU'VE
MISSED THE VERY REASON FOR
YOUR OWN EXISTENCE.

ADDITIONAL RESOURCES

J. I. Packer, *Knowing God*, InterVarsity Press, 1993.

John Piper, *Desiring God*, Multnomah Publishers, 1996.

John Stott, *Basic Christianity*, Rev. Ed., Wm. B. Eerdmans Publishing Co., 1986.

A. W. Tozer, *Pursuit of God*, Christian Publications, 1982.

A. W. Tozer, *The Knowledge of the Holy*, Harper, San Francisco, 1978.

SESSION TWO

The Truth About You

PART ONE
UNDERSTANDING THE PROBLEM

A quarter-century ago, psychiatrist Karl Menninger wrote a landmark book titled *Whatever Became of Sin?* There are many answers to that question, but this one is certainly true: Nothing has happened to sin, but something has happened to us. We simply don't want to talk about sin anymore. It isn't a polite topic, especially not in polite society. Try mentioning the word "sin" the next time you go to a party and see how long it takes for someone to change the subject.

But our avoiding the subject doesn't change the truth. Something has gone wrong with the human race. No one can successfully deny that fact. We are not all that we could be. And no matter how much we boast of our technological achievements, the fact of man's inhumanity to man always grabs the front page. The details change, the faces come and go, but the story is always the same. Something evil lurks inside the heart of every person. No one is immune, no one is exempt, and no one is truly innocent. Call it what you will—a twist, a taint, a bent to do wrong. Somehow, somewhere, someone injected poison into the human bloodstream. That's why, even when we know the right thing to do, we often go ahead and choose to do wrong. Deliberately. Repeatedly. Defiantly.

The world is a mess—we all know that. The world is a mess because we ourselves are messed up. The problem is not "out there." It's "in us." The world is bad because we are bad. The world is evil because evil lurks within us.

If that assessment of the human predicament seems harsh, stay tuned. In this session we're going to discover the bad news that will lead us to the good news.

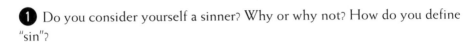

A QUICK QUIZ

1 Do you consider yourself a sinner? Why or why not? How do you define "sin"?

2 Do you believe most people are basically good or basically bad? Explain your answer.

3 What do the following verses teach about . . .

The condition of your heart—Jeremiah 17:9

Our natural inclination—Isaiah 53:6

The universal nature of sin—Romans 3:23

The wages of sin—Romans 6:23

Rate yourself on the following scale from 1–10:

1	2	3	4	5	6	7	8	9	1 0

Definitely   About average   Better than
a sinner   most people

Extra credit: How would the people who know you best rate you?
Hint: Ask them!

PART TWO ～
THE TEN COMMANDMENTS AND YOU

The Ten Commandments are found in Exodus 20:1–17. These commandments reveal God's standard of judgment for the whole human race. How well do you stack
up against this list? Before you answer, remember that, since God is perfect, He demands perfection. He doesn't "grade on a curve." He won't compare you to anyone
else—a friend, a family member, or your next-door neighbor. God demands perfect
performance all the time. Think about that as you read through this list.

After each description, give yourself a score ranging from 1 (often broken this
commandment) to 3 (usually keep this commandment) to 5 (have always obeyed
this commandment in letter and in spirit perfectly). Circle the number that represents your most honest self-evaluation.

The First Commandment: NO OTHER GODS (Exodus 20:1–3)
This means exclusive loyalty to God alone as the Lord of your life. It demands
that you love the Lord with all your heart and mind and soul and strength, and
that you serve Him through worship and obedience.

How I rate myself on the First Commandment: 1   2   3   4   5

The Second Commandment: NO IDOLS (Exodus 20:4–6)
This prohibits dabbling in false religions, witchcraft, sorcery, fortune telling,
and the New Age movement, and any attempts to blend Christianity with other
religions. On a broader scale, anything good that becomes a controlling force in
my life can become an idol. If my devotion to my job or my family or my
friends or my plans and dreams or the things I own is greater than my devotion
to God, those good things have become idols to me. Most modern idols are
good things that have become too important to us.

How I rate myself on the Second Commandment: 1   2   3   4   5

The Third Commandment: DO NOT USE GOD'S NAME IN VAIN
(Exodus 20:7)
This means showing deep respect for who God is—in your words and by the
way you live. It rules out using God's name as a swear word and it also rules out
blasphemy, careless speech, and flippant jokes involving God. On the positive

side, it demands that we take God seriously—not just on Sunday but every day of the week.

How I rate myself on the Third Commandment: 1   2   3   4   5

The Fourth Commandment: KEEP THE SABBATH DAY HOLY
(Exodus 20:8–11)

God wants us to honor Him by setting aside time each week for rest and worship. This rules out the workaholic spirit that says, "I can do it all." It forces us to acknowledge that all we have comes from the Lord and that we are totally dependent on Him for everything. Obeying this commandment involves generous giving of our time, talent, and treasure to God and to those in need. Instead of hoarding up our wealth, we live for others.

How I rate myself on the Fourth Commandment: 1   2   3   4   5

The Fifth Commandment: HONOR YOUR FATHER AND MOTHER
(Exodus 20:12)

We are called to honor and respect our parents by what we say and do. This applies even if our parents were less than ideal or even if they were absent or unkind to us. Once we leave home, we may not always obey our parents, but we are always under an obligation to love, honor, and respect them—even after their death. This involves remembering them in their old age, speaking well of them when we can, and refusing to speak evil of them to others. We will make every effort to care for our parents and to protect their reputation as much as possible.

How I rate myself on the Fifth Commandment: 1   2   3   4   5

The Sixth Commandment: DO NOT MURDER (Exodus 20:13)

This covers the killing of innocent human life. It also covers the hatred and bitterness that leads to murderous attitudes in the heart (Matthew 5:21–26). It rules out rage, malice, physical violence, threats, intimidation, abusive behavior, slander, racial and ethnic hatred, all forms of abusive language, and the wrong attitudes from which these things spring. Uncontrolled anger is murder in the heart.

How I rate myself on the Sixth Commandment: 1   2   3   4   5

The Seventh Commandment: DO NOT COMMIT ADULTERY
(Exodus 20:14)

God's standard is moral purity before marriage and moral purity within marriage. This rules out pornography, all forms of lust-provoking entertainment, homosexuality, all premarital and extra-marital sex, and all filthy language, suggestive behavior, and immodest dress. If you harbor lust in your heart, you have broken this commandment (Matthew 5:28).

How I rate myself on the Seventh Commandment: 1   2   3   4   5

The Eighth Commandment: DO NOT STEAL (Exodus 20:15)

This involves having respect for the property of others. We are not to steal what belongs to another person. This includes stealing property, time, or even another person's reputation.

How I rate myself on the Eighth Commandment: 1   2   3   4   5

The Ninth Commandment: DO NOT GIVE FALSE TESTIMONY
(Exodus 20:16)

This commandment prohibits perjury, slander, and libel. It also covers gossip, malicious talk, spreading rumors, telling the truth with the sole purpose of injuring someone's reputation, unkind exaggeration, harmful teasing, racist remarks, hateful speech, unkind comments, rude retorts, sullen obedience, rebellious speech, and any sort of misinformation designed to gain a personal advantage over another person.

How I rate myself on the Ninth Commandment: 1   2   3   4   5

The Tenth Commandment: DO NOT COVET (Exodus 20:17)

On one hand, this commandment teaches us to be content with what we have. It also touches our heart attitude toward those around us who have what we do not. It rules out jealous and envy. When we break this commandment by our wrong attitudes, it usually leads us to break other commandments as well. (See Romans 7:7–12.)

How I rate myself on the Tenth Commandment: 1   2   3   4   5

THE TEN COMMANDMENTS PERFECTION TEST

Since God demands perfection, the following test involves answering *Yes* or *No* to each question. You can answer *Yes* to any question if you have kept that commandment perfectly in thought, word, and deed, with no deviation whatsoever, with no wrong attitudes, and with perfect compliance outwardly and inwardly from the day of your birth until now. Remember: The slightest failure at any point along the way means you must answer *No*.

I have perfectly kept the First Commandment: ❑ Yes   ❑ No

I have perfectly kept the Second Commandment: ❑ Yes   ❑ No

I have perfectly kept the Third Commandment: ❑ Yes   ❑ No

I have perfectly kept the Fourth Commandment: ❑ Yes   ❑ No

I have perfectly kept the Fifth Commandment: ❑ Yes   ❑ No

I have perfectly kept the Sixth Commandment: ❑ Yes   ❑ No

I have perfectly kept the Seventh Commandment: ❑ Yes   ❑ No

I have perfectly kept the Eighth Commandment: ❑ Yes   ❑ No

I have perfectly kept the Ninth Commandment: ❑ Yes   ❑ No

I have perfectly kept the Tenth Commandment: ❑ Yes   ❑ No

Scoring Key: Count the number of Yes answers and the number of No answers. Then grade as follows:

10 *Yes* answers: PASS

1–10 *No* answers: FAIL

That's right. If you answered *No* to just one question, you fail the entire test. God demands 100 percent perfection to all His commandments all the time. If you break even one commandment one time, to God it's as if you broke all of them all the time. (See James 2:10–11.)

PART THREE ◦—
THE EXCUSES WE MAKE

Part of our problem is that it's easy for us to confess someone else's sins. The tendency toward hypocrisy shows itself in many subtle ways. Have you ever noticed how we like to "rename" our sins? We do that by ascribing the worst motives to others, while using other phrases to let ourselves off the hook. If you do it, you're a liar; I merely "stretch the truth." If you do it, you're cheating; I am "bending the rules."

You lose your temper; *I have righteous anger.*
You're a jerk; *I'm having a bad day.*
You curse and swear; *I let off steam.*
You're pushy; *I'm intensely goal-oriented.*
You're greedy; *I'm simply taking care of business.*
You're a hypochondriac; *I'm really sick.*
You stink; *I merely have an "earthy aroma."*

—◦ *The tendency to blame others started a long time ago. According to Genesis 3:9–12, how did Adam respond when God confronted him about his sin?*

—◦ *Can you think of other examples of how we either minimize our own sin or shift the blame to others?*

For each of the following statements, write "Agree" or "Do not agree" or "Not sure."

_____ God is very angry with me because of my sin.

_____ Everything is fine between me and God.

_____ God knows I'm doing the best I can right now.

_____ I'm not perfect, but I wouldn't call myself a sinner.

_____ Most of my problems are not really my fault.

_____ If I'm good enough, God will forgive my sins.

_____ I don't worry about God and He doesn't worry about me.

+ +

_____ God loves me in spite of my sin.

_____ I don't believe in the concept of sin.

_____ I'm a sinner! There's no question about that.

PART FOUR ∘—
THE CONSEQUENCES OF SIN

What do the following verses teach about our true condition apart from God's grace?

Luke 19:10 *We are _____ .*

Ephesians 2:1–2 *We are spiritually _____ .*

Isaiah 59:2 *We are _____ from God.*

Titus 3:3 *We are _____ to sin.*

2 Corinthians 4:4 *We are spiritually _____ .*

John 3:18 *We are _____ already.*

2 Timothy 2:26 *We are held _____ by Satan.*

John 3:36 *We face the _____ of God.*

Ephesians 2:12 *We are without _____ in the world.*

1 Corinthians 2:14 *We lack spiritual _____ .*

Romans 5:6 *We were _____ to change our condition.*

—∘ *In light of these verses, how would you answer someone who says, "I may be a sinner, but I'm not that bad off. I can handle my problems on my own"?*

✦ ✦

PERSONAL QUESTIONS: Do you believe in heaven and hell? Why or why not? How certain are you about this? If you died right now, where would go: heaven, hell, or somewhere else? How important is it to you to know the answer to the last question?

A VERSE TO MEMORIZE

"For all have sinned and fall short
of the glory of God."
— Romans 3:23 ESV

A PRAYER FOR THOSE WILLING TO FACE THE TRUTH

Gracious Father, thank You for showing me the truth about myself. I confess that I am a sinner in Your eyes. Too many times I have gone my own way and have ignored Your commands. I have not done what I should have done, and I have many times said and done things that I knew were wrong in Your sight. I am tired of making excuses and blaming others instead of taking personal responsibility for my sin.

Apart from Your grace, I have no hope of salvation in this life or the life to come. Thank You for providing a way where sinners like me can find forgiveness and a brand-new life. In Jesus' name. Amen.

A Truth to Remember

THE ONLY PEOPLE WHO THINK
THEY ARE GOOD ENOUGH TO
GO TO HEAVEN ARE THE
PEOPLE WHO DON'T KNOW
HOW BAD THEY REALLY ARE.

✢ ✢

ADDITIONAL RESOURCES

Alistair Begg, *What Angels Wish They Knew*, Moody Press, 1998.

John Bunyan and Warren Wiersbe, *The New Pilgrim's Progress*, Discovery House Publishing, 1989.

C. S. Lewis, *Mere Christianity*, Harper San Francisco, 2001.

Dallas Willard, *The Divine Conspiracy*, Harper San Francisco Publishing, 1998.

Ravi Zacharias, *Can Man Live Without God?*, Word Publishing, 1996.

— SESSION THREE —
Amazing Grace

PART ONE —
GOOD NEWS FOR SINNERS

In his book *What's So Amazing About Grace?* Philip Yancey comments that grace is the "last great word." He means that it is one of the last of the old English words that has retained something of its original meaning: "free and undeserved bounty." He points out that when we pray, we "say grace" to thank God for our food. We are "grateful" for a kindness shown by another person. To show our thanks we offer a "gratuity." Something that is offered at no cost is said to be "gratis." And when we have overdue books from the library, we may return them without penalty during a "grace period."

It is commonly said that Christianity is supremely a religion of grace. And that is certainly true. We sing about grace, we write poems about grace, we name our churches and our children after grace. But for all that, grace is not well understood and often not really believed. We use the word a great deal but rarely think about what it means. Part of our problem is in the nature of grace itself. Grace is scandalous. Hard to accept. Hard to believe. Hard to receive. We all have a certain skepticism when a telemarketer tells us, "I'm not trying to sell you anything. I just want to offer you a free trip to Hawaii." Automatically we wonder, "What's the catch?" because we have been taught that there's no free lunch.

Grace shocks us in what it offers. It is truly not of this world. It frightens us because of what it does for sinners. Grace teaches us that God does for others what we would never do for them. We would save the not-so-bad. God starts with prostitutes and then works downward from there. Grace is a gift that costs everything to the giver and nothing to the receiver. It is given to those who don't deserve it, barely recognize it, and hardly appreciate it.

In this session, we'll discover what grace means, why we need it, and how we can encounter the free grace of God. If you prefer justice to grace, you may not enjoy this session. But if grace sounds good to you, let's jump in and get started.

—◦ *Give a simple definition of the word "grace."*

—◦ *Do you believe God loves you? Why or why not?*

—◦ *As far as you can tell, what is the essential difference between Christianity and every other religion in the world?*

A SIMPLE PRAYER FOR GOD'S GRACE

As we begin, here's a simple prayer: "Lord, show me the power of Your grace today! Amen." When we open ourselves to God's amazing grace, we're going to be amazed at how God answers us.

PART TWO ⌒
A CLOSER LOOK AT GRACE

Ephesians 2:1–10 offers one of the clearest explanations of grace in the Bible. The following questions are based on this passage.

—◦ *According to verses 1–2, what words or phrases describe our true condition before we come to Christ for salvation?*

—◦ *If those without Christ are spiritually dead, why do they sometimes appear to be happy and fulfilled even though they don't know the Lord?*

—◦ *Take a look at the phrase "followed the ways of this world" in verse 2. What does that suggest to you? What does that mean in 21st-century terms?*

✢ ✢

—❧ *Verses 4–5 mention three words that describe God's action toward us: love, mercy, and grace. Briefly define each word as it relates to God.*

—❧ *If salvation is by grace and not by works (verses 8–9), why do so many people think they have to do good works in order to go to heaven?*

—❧ *What place do good works have once you come by faith to the Lord Jesus Christ (verse 10)?*

📖 THE BIBLE IN YOUR OWN WORDS

In order to understand this passage better, paraphrase it in your own words, using first-person pronouns. For instance, verse 1 might become,

"Before I came to Christ, I was spiritually dead. I ignored God's commands and lived as a sinner. Back then, God wasn't part of my life."

Let this passage be part of your own spiritual journey. Tell it in your own words. Since you aren't writing Scripture to be read in church, make it very personal.

PART THREE ~
HOW A TERRORIST BECAME AN EVANGELIST

Read Acts 8:1–3 and Galatians 1:13–24. Note: The "Saul" of Acts 8 and "Paul" of Galatians 1 refer to the same person.

1 According to Galatians 1:13–14, what was Paul's spiritual condition before he came to Christ? How did he feel about Christians and about the Christian church?

2 When did God first start working in Paul's life (verse 15)? Who made the first move—Paul or God?

3 How did the Christian churches respond when they heard about Paul's conversion (verses 22–24)?

PERSONAL QUESTIONS: Can you think of a time in your life, good or bad, when you felt a need to know God personally? Can you think of a time when you sensed that God was at work in your life, drawing you to Himself?

"Christianity is supremely a religion of conversion. It is built upon one fundamental and revolutionary premise: You don't have to stay the way you are. Your life can be radically changed by God. Conversion is a miracle that happens when the life of God intersects with human personality. Religion is one thing; conversion is something else entirely. It is the conviction that long-held prejudices can be overcome, lifetime habits can be broken, and deeply ingrained patterns of sin can be erased over time. Conversion is the certainty that what you were does not determine what you are, and what you are does not determine what you will be. You can be changed, you can be different, your life can move in an entirely new direction."

✢ ✢

—✧ *Which parts of your life need to be "radically changed by God?"*

PART FOUR ✍
YOUR SPIRITUAL JOURNEY SO FAR

Check as many of the following statements that apply to you right now.

- ❑ I'm okay just the way I am.
- ❑ I believe if I do my best, everything will work out and I'll end up in heaven.
- ❑ I'm not sure I can trust what the Bible says.
- ❑ I'm bothered by the fact that some people will end up in heaven and others will end up in hell forever. That doesn't seem right to me.
- ❑ I truly want to know God better.
- ❑ I believe that all religions basically teach the same thing.
- ❑ To me it's narrow-minded to say that Jesus is the only way to heaven.
- ❑ You don't have to convince me that I'm a sinner. I know that already.
- ❑ I'm not sure what will happen to me when I die.
- ❑ Unless I see a miracle with my own eyes, I'm never going to believe in Jesus.
- ❑ I want to know Jesus personally.

TWO QUICK QUESTIONS

❶ On the basis of what we have studied so far, what is God's solution to the sin problem that affects the entire human race?

❷ How do you react to the teaching that there is nothing at all you can do to save yourself and that salvation is a free gift from God and must be received by faith alone?

A VERSE TO MEMORIZE

"For by grace you have been saved through faith. And this is not your own doing; it is the gift of God, not a result of works, so that no one may boast."

—⟳ Ephesians 2:8–9 ESV

A PRAYER FOR GOD'S GRACE

Father, You created me and You know the full truth about me. You know me completely and absolutely. Nothing is hidden from Your eyes. Thank You for the grace that reaches down to me even though I am a sinner in thought and word and deed. I confess that I too often do those things that I said I would not do, and I do not do those things I said I would do. Help me, Lord! I want to know You deeply and personally. Without Your grace I am hopelessly lost, but I know that by Your grace all things are possible. May the Lord Jesus Christ be revealed in my life. Do whatever it takes that I might know You. Amen.

A Truth to Remember

GRACE NEVER GOES UP; IT ALWAYS COMES DOWN. GRACE BY DEFINITION MEANS THAT GOD GIVES US WHAT WE DON'T DESERVE AND COULD NEVER EARN.

✣ ✣

ADDITIONAL RESOURCES

Max Lucado, *In the Grip of Grace*, Word Publishing, 1996.

Max Lucado, *The Gift for All People*, Multnomah Publishers, 1999.

Charles H. Spurgeon, *All of Grace*, Moody Press, n.d.

Charles Swindoll, *The Grace Awakening*, Word Publishing, 1996.

Philip Yancey, *What's So Amazing About Grace?* Zondervan Publishing House, 1997.

—◦ SESSION FOUR ◦—
A Man Called Jesus

PART ONE ◦—
WILL THE REAL JESUS PLEASE STAND UP?

Who is Jesus Christ? Before you answer that question, let me set the scene. It's a few minutes past noon in downtown Philadelphia. You're walking with a few friends to a favorite lunch spot when a camera crew stops you for a spontaneous interview. To your surprise, their questions have nothing to do with the White House, politics, the economy, or where you stand on capital punishment. The interviewer wants to know what you think about Jesus Christ. Who is He? While you fumble for an answer, the video camera records your discomfort. You weren't prepared for this, much less dressed for it, and now you're being quizzed on theology while your friends watch from five feet away. The seconds pass as various answers flash across your mental screen: "A good man ... The Son of God ... A prophet ... A Galilean rabbi ... A teacher of God's law ... The embodiment of God's love ... A reincarnated spirit master ... The ultimate revolutionary ... The Messiah of Israel ... Savior ... A first-century wise man ... A man just like any other man ... King of kings ... A misunderstood teacher ... Lord of the universe ... A fool who thought he was God's Son ... Son of Man ... A fabrication of the early church."

Which answer will you give? Before you answer, let me say that you can find people today who will give every one of those possible answers. But it's nothing new. When Jesus asked His disciples, "Who do people say I am?" they replied with four different answers (see Matthew 16:13–16). Even when He walked on this Earth, people were confused as to His true identity. Some thought He was a prophet, others a great political leader, still others thought He was John the Baptist come back to life.

Who is Jesus Christ? Or to borrow a phrase from television, will the real Jesus please stand up? The only way to discover the real Jesus is to go the original source—the Bible.

Listed below are some of the modern explanations of Jesus Christ. Check the ones you've heard or read about. Add any others you can think of.

- ❑ Good man
- ❑ Son of God
- ❑ Jewish rabbi
- ❑ Teacher of God's Law
- ❑ Messiah of Israel
- ❑ Ultimate revolutionary
- ❑ Reincarnated spirit master
- ❑ Holy man but not the Son of God
- ❑ He never existed at all

—◦ *Which of the above options would you say is definitely NOT true about Jesus? Why? What is your basis for making that judgment?*

—◦ *How do you account for the continuing popularity of Jesus Christ?*

PART TWO
BEFORE ABRAHAM WAS, I AM

"Your father Abraham rejoiced at the thought of seeing my day; he saw it and was glad." "You are not yet fifty years old," the Jews said to him, "and you have seen Abraham!" "I tell you the truth," Jesus answered, "before Abraham was born, I am!" (John 8:56–58).

- The "deity of Christ" means that Jesus was truly and actually God in human flesh. To see Him was to see God.
- "I AM" was the name by which God identified Himself in Exodus 3:14.
- Though He was born as a man, in John 8:56–58 Jesus claims to have existed before Abraham. His opponents understood this as a claim to deity. That's why they attempted to stone Him (verse 59).

—◦ *What is the chief stumbling block that keeps people from believing that Jesus was God in human flesh? If you personally don't believe or are not sure that Jesus was truly God, how do you account for what He said and did?*

—◦ *What are the implications for all of humanity if Jesus truly was God?*

—◦ *If Jesus is who He said He was, what are the implications of rejecting that truth (John 8:24)?*

SEVEN FACTS ABOUT JESUS YOU NEED TO KNOW!

1 He had a supernatural entrance into the world (Matthew 1:18–25).

2 He was God in human flesh (John 1:14).

3 He is the standard of absolute righteousness (Hebrews 4:15).

4 He did things only God can do (Luke 5:17–26).

5 He died as a sacrifice for our sins (Mark 10:45).

6 He proved His claims by rising from the dead (Matthew 28:5–6).

7 He will one day return to the earth (John 14:1–3).

11 P.M. IN THE DORM

You and your roommate at the university have had many late-night discussions about religion. The key question always comes back to this: Who is Jesus Christ? She can't believe that Jesus is the only way of salvation and that outside of Christ no one goes to heaven. That seems cruel and unfair to her. What do you say in response?

✢ ✢

PART THREE ⌒
CHECK OUT HIS MIRACLES

When John the Baptist was in prison, he sent his disciples to Jesus with a very poignant question: "Are you the one who was to come or should we expect someone else?" (Matthew 11:3). Jesus answered by listing the miracles He had performed: the blind see, the lame walk, the deaf hear, the lepers are cleansed, and the dead are raised. No one could fake such miracles as that. No religious charlatan could give sight to the blind. Not even the great Houdini could raise the dead. Only the mighty Son of God could work such stupendous miracles.

Here are some of them:

Turned water into _____ (John 2:1–11)

Multiplied the _____ and fish (John 6:5–13)

Walked on _____ (Matthew 14:25)

Opened the eyes of a _____ man (John 9)

Made the lame _____ (Matthew 9:1–8)

Cast out _____ (Mark 5:1–20)

Stilled a raging _____ (Mark 4:35–41)

Cleansed ten _____ (Luke 17:11–19)

Raised the _____ (Matthew 9:18–26)

—⌒ *What was the overall purpose of His miracles?* (See John 3:1–2 and Acts 2:22.)

—⌒ *Did everyone who saw His miracles believe in Him? Why or why not?* (See Matthew 11:20 and 12:22–24.)

PART FOUR ⌒
THE CLAIMS OF CHRIST

Here is a fact not often appreciated by the nonreligious person. Jesus made abolutely astounding claims concerning Himself. In fact, if you catalogue His own words, you must conclude that either He is who He said He was or else is a liar or a madman. The people who say, "Jesus was a good man—nothing more" have never read the gospels, because you could never come to that conclusion if you actually read what Jesus said about Himself.

What claims did Jesus make about Himself?

I am the _____ of life (John 6:48).

I am the _____ of the world (John 8:12).

I am from _____ (John 8:23).

I am the good _____ (John 10:11).

I am the _____ and the _____ (John 11:25).

I am the _____, the _____, and the _____ (John 14:6).

In other passages, He claimed that He was the Son of God (John 3:16), that the angels obeyed Him (Matthew 13:41), that He could forgive sin (Luke 5:20), and that He could raise people from the dead (John 5:25). He even claimed to be the source of eternal life (John 10:28). These are absolutely stupendous claims. If He is not who He claimed to be, then He is certainly not a mere man. He is either a liar or seriously deluded or perhaps something worse than that. But if these claims are true, then He must truly be God in human flesh. Immanuel—God with us. If Jesus is who He said He is, there is no truth more worthy of your time, no person more important to know. Who is Jesus Christ? Spend a moment thinking about how you would respond. Your answer determines your eternal destiny.

THINK ABOUT IT!

In what way is Jesus different from every other religious leader in history? What evidence backs up the astounding claims He made for Himself?

THE "WHO IS JESUS?" CHALLENGE

*F*ind someone who is not a Christian and ask them what they think about Jesus Christ. Who is He? Where did He come from? Can His words be trusted? Tell that person what the Bible says about Jesus Christ. Take a moment and pray right now. Ask God to show you who He wants you to talk to about Jesus. If a name comes to mind, write that name in the space below.

I believe God wants me to talk to _____ *about Jesus this week.*

A VERSE TO MEMORIZE

"And this is eternal life, that they know you the only true God, and Jesus Christ whom you have sent"
—⚓ John 17:3 ESV

A PRAYER FOR SPIRITUAL INSIGHT

Heavenly Father, You said, "Let there be light," and light came into the world. You see all things as they truly are. Search my heart, O Lord. Open my eyes that I may see the truth. If Jesus truly is the Son of God, if He truly died for me, help me to see it and help me to know Him. I seek the light that leads to eternal life with You. May that light now shine in my heart. Amen.

> ## A Truth to Remember
>
> THE CHRISTIAN CHURCH IS
> MADE UP OF MEN AND
> WOMEN WHO CONFESS ONE
> REVOLUTIONARY TRUTH:
> THAT JESUS OF NAZARETH IS
> THE SON OF THE LIVING GOD.

ADDITIONAL RESOURCES

Erwin Lutzer, *Christ Among Other Gods*, Moody Press, 1997.

Josh McDowell, *More Than a Carpenter*, Tyndale House Publishers, 1987.

Joseph M. Stowell, *Simply Jesus*, Multnomah Publishers, 2002.

Lee Strobel, *The Case for Christ*, Zondervan Publishing House, 1998.

Ravi Zacharias, *Jesus Among Other Gods*, Word Publishing, 2000.

✢ ✢

✎ SESSION FIVE ✎

It is Finished

PART ONE ✎

HE DIED ON GOOD FRIDAY

Friday morning in Jerusalem. Another hot April day. Death is in the air. Word has spread to every corner of the city. The Romans plan to crucify somebody today. The crucifixion begins at nine o'clock sharp. The Romans are punctual about things like that. At first the crowd is rowdy, loud, raucous, boisterous, as if this were some kind of athletic event. They cheer, they laugh, they shout, they place wagers on how long the men being crucified will last. It appears that the man in the middle will not last long. He has already been severely beaten. In fact, it looks as though four or five soldiers have taken turns working Him over. His skin hangs from his back in tatters, His face is bruised and swollen, His eyes nearly shut. Blood trickles from a dozen open wounds. He is an awful sight to behold.

At noon "darkness fell upon all the land." It happened so suddenly that no one expected it. One moment the sun was right overhead; the next moment it had disappeared. It was not an eclipse nor was it a dark cloud cover. It was darkness itself, thick, inky-black darkness that fell like a shroud over the land. It was darkness without any hint of light to come. It was chilling blackness that curdled the blood and froze the skin.

At 3 P.M., just as suddenly as the darkness had descended, it disappeared. All eyes focus on the center cross. It is clear the end is near. Jesus is at the point of death. Whatever happened in those three hours of darkness has brought Him to death's door. His strength is nearly gone, the struggle almost over. His chest heaves with every tortured breath; His moans now are only whispers. Instinctively the crowd pushes closer to watch His last moments.

Then it happened. He shouted something—"My God, my God, why have you forsaken me?" Someone in the crowd shouted back to Him. Moments passed, death drew near, then a hoarse whisper, "I thirst." The soldiers put some sour vinegar on a sponge and lift it to His lips with a stalk of hyssop. He moistened His lips and took a deep breath. If you listened you could hear the death rattle in His throat. He had less than a minute to live. Then He spoke again. It was a quick shout. Just one word.

If you weren't paying attention, you missed it in all the confusion. He breathed out another sentence. Then He was dead.

What does the cross of Christ mean to you? In this session we'll take a close look at the death of Christ. Ask the Lord to help you see Christ as you've never seen Him before.

—◦ *What words or phrases come to mind when you think of the word "crucify"?*

—◦ *How many people would you die for right now, on a moment's notice, no questions asked?*

—◦ *Do you believe that God loves you? Why or why not?*

YOU WERE THERE!

Find a modern translation of the Bible and read John 18–19 out loud. The impact of Jesus' crucifixion will become more real to you as you hear yourself telling the story of the death of Jesus Christ.

PART TWO ◦—
PREDICTED AND FULFILLED

One of the most amazing proofs of the divine inspiration of the Bible is that it records in great detail the many prophecies surrounding the death of Jesus Christ. These prophecies were first made hundreds of years before Christ was born. Listed below are some of the Old Testament prophecies regarding the death of Christ and their New Testament fulfillment. Jot down beside each one the event that was predicted and fulfilled.

Psalm 41:9 and Luke 22:3–5 _____

Zechariah 11:12 and Matthew 26:14–16 _____

Isaiah 53:3 and Matthew 27:29–31 _____

Isaiah 53:7 and Mark 14:61 _____

Psalm 22:16 and John 20:25 _____

✠ ✠

Psalm 22:18 and Mark 15:24 _____

Psalm 34:20 and John 19:33, 36 _____

Zechariah 12:10 and John 19:34 _____

Isaiah 53:9 and Luke 23:50–53 _____

⇨ *How do you account for these fulfilled prophecies surrounding the death of Christ?*

> ❏ Just chance or coincidence
>
> ❏ It was written to make it look like a fulfillment
>
> ❏ Too vague to be literal fulfillment
>
> ❏ Prophecies fulfilled as part of God's plan

WHO KILLED JESUS?

Here's a question for personal investigation: Who killed Jesus? That is, who is ultimately responsible for His death? Over the centuries, some have blamed the Jews and used that as an excuse for persecuting the Jewish people. Did the Jews kill Jesus? Or were the Romans ultimately responsible? If His death was part of God's plan to bring salvation to the world, then isn't God responsible for the death of His Son? But if He died for our sins, aren't we partly responsible for Jesus' death? Check out these Scriptures while you are working on your answer: Isaiah 53:6, 10; Matthew 26:3–4; Matthew 27:22–26; John 10:17–18; Acts 2:22–23; Acts 3:18.

PART THREE ☙
WHY DID JESUS HAVE TO DIE?

Many people stumble over the concept of a crucified Savior. Some think it is silly, others meaningless, still others find it offensive and even repulsive. Occasionally critics have called Christianity a "slaughterhouse religion" because of the central emphasis on the bloody death of Jesus Christ. In one sense, the criticism is correct in that the cross is at the very center of our faith. Take out the cross of Christ and Christianity ceases to be a supernatural religion.

That Jesus died is a fact of history. But why did He die? What did His death accomplish? And did He have to die? Before we go further, take a moment and check the statement that best expresses your current understanding of the death of Jesus Christ:

❑ He died as a martyr who was crucified because He was a threat to the powers-that-be.

❑ He died to offer us a model of a man supremely dedicated to God.

❑ He died in our place, taking our sins upon Himself, and bearing the punishment for our sins.

❑ He died as a moral example to show us how to live and how to die.

❑ He died in order to unite the world in a religion of eternal love.

❑ He died because He was a sinner just like anyone else.

Here are some verses that will help us understand why Christ had to die on the cross:

- What is the wages of sin? (Romans 6:23; see also Revelation 21:8)
- Even our good deeds are like what in the eyes of God? (Isaiah 64:6)
- According to Hebrews 9:22, what is required for the forgiveness of sin?
- 1 Timothy 2:6 tells us that Christ died as a _____ for all. Jot down what you think that means.
- According to Isaiah 53:6, what happened to our sins when Christ died?
- If Christ took our sin upon himself, what do we receive in exchange? (2 Corinthians 5:21)
- What does the blood of Jesus Christ do for us? (1 John 1:7)
- Hebrews 2:14 says that through his death, Jesus thoroughly defeated the one who had the power of death, that is, the _____.

"HE DIED FOR ME"

What does the death of Christ mean to you personally? Think about His death and your life. Do you see any connection? Write your answers in the space below.

✛ ✛

Think about it this way:

- God is holy and righteous.
- Our sins are an offense to our holy God.
- Sin must be punished fully and completely.
- The punishment for sin is always death.
- Either we pay the price or someone pays it for us.
- Christ came to pay the full price for our sins.
- He died in our place, taking our punishment.
- The wrath of God that should have fallen on us fell instead on Him.
- Those who believe on Him as Lord and Savior will never perish.
- For those who do not believe on Him, there is only eternal punishment.

But this Man, after he had offered one sacrifice for sins forever, sat down at the right hand of God" (Hebrews 10:12 NKJV). Jesus cried out, "It is finished" (John 19:30 NKJV), because the work of salvation was complete. His death was the full payment for our sins. He bore our sins in His own body on the cross, dying as the perfect Son of God for the sins of the world. His one sacrifice paid in full the penalty for our sin. He is now seated at the Father's right hand in heaven because He finished the work of salvation at the cross 2,000 years ago.

PART FOUR ❧
NAME YOUR SIN

What sin is keeping you from God right now? Here is some good news. It doesn't matter what "your" sin is. It doesn't matter how guilty you think you are. When you come to Christ, you discover that all of your sins have been stamped by God with this phrase: Paid in full.

Anger	Paid in Full
Uncontrolled ambition	Paid in Full
Gossip	Paid in Full
Drunkenness	Paid in Full
Fornication	Paid in Full
Embezzlement	Paid in Full

Lying . . . . .Paid in Full

Disobedience . . . . .Paid in Full

Slothfulness . . . . .Paid in Full

Pride . . . . .Paid in Full

Murder . . . . .Paid in Full

Bribery . . . . .Paid in Full

_____ . . . . .Paid in Full

_____ . . . . .Paid in Full

_____ . . . . .Paid in Full

_____ . . . . .Paid in Full

Fill in the blanks with other sins in your life. Through the blood of Jesus Christ the price for "your" sins has been Paid in Full.

A VERSE TO MEMORIZE

"All we like sheep have gone astray; we have turned every one to his own way; and the Lord has laid on him the iniquity of us all."
Isaiah 53:6 ESV

A PRAYER TO CHRIST THE SAVIOR

Lord Jesus, I bow before Your holy cross where Your blood was shed for me. I bless You, Son of God and God the Son, that You died in my place, taking my sin, bearing my shame, enduring the insults of sinful men. This You did not only for me but for the entire world. Show me my sin more clearly that I might love You more dearly. I rejoice because Your justice is satisfied and the price for sin has been paid in full. Grant me faith to lay hold of the cross as my salvation that I may say with full assurance, "When Jesus died, He died for me." Amen.

A Truth to Remember

WHAT JESUS ACCOMPLISHED
IN HIS DEATH WAS SO
AWESOME, SO TOTAL, SO
COMPLETE THAT IT COULD
NEVER BE REPEATED, NOT
EVEN BY JESUS HIMSELF.

ADDITIONAL RESOURCES

James Montgomery Boice and Philip Graham Ryken, *The Heart of the Cross*, Crossway Books, 1999.

Erwin Lutzer, *Cries from the Cross*, Moody Press, 2002.

John MacArthur, *The Murder of Jesus*, Word Publishing, 2001.

Ray Pritchard, *In the Shadow of the Cross*, Broadman & Holman, 2001.

John Stott, *The Cross of Christ*, InterVarsity Press, 1986.

✛ .

—◦ SESSION SIX ◦—
The Great Exchange

PART ONE ◦—
THE HEART OF THE GOSPEL

What's your credit like with God? If God is the Great Creditor, are you "in the red" or "in the black" as far as He is concerned? That question came to mind one day as I opened my mail at home. As I sorted the envelopes into two piles, it seemed as if everything we received that day was either a credit card bill or an invitation to apply for more credit cards. Some of the invitations were quite seductive. Low interest rates, the opportunity to get "free" merchandise and special super-discounts on certain items that I would probably never buy at any price.

Let's take the concept of credit into the spiritual realm. How much credit do you have with God? The Bible offers a surprising answer to that question. We are all born spiritually bankrupt and spend our lives overdrawing on an account that is already far gone "in the red." But because of what Christ accomplished on the cross, God allows bankrupt sinners who have no hope of credit-worthiness, to "borrow" whatever they need based on His Son's unlimited credit in heaven. Then God pays the statement once for all! This is how we can get our lives out of spiritual debt and end up on the plus side of the ledger.

With this session we have finally arrived at the heart of the Good News. We have already seen that, when Jesus died, He paid in full for our sins. How does that apply to you and me? The answer is that God justifies wicked people who trust in Him. He credits their account in heaven with the righteousness of Jesus Christ. Thus, the guilty are acquitted on the basis of what Jesus Christ did when He died on the cross and rose from the dead.

◦ *If you were God, what would you require from sinful men and women before you let them into heaven?*

—◦ *Suppose you died tonight and found yourself at the gate of heaven. How would you answer if God said to you, "Why should I let you into My heaven?"*

Finish this sentence: "If God graded my life thus far, I would probably get a(n) _____."

PART TWO ◦—
STRAIGHT TALK ABOUT JUSTIFICATION

The word "justify" means "to declare righteous." It's a legal term that comes from the courtrooms of the first century. When a judge pronounced a verdict of "not guilty," the accused was free to go. No charges against him were kept on the record. In the eyes of the law, he was justified or acquitted. No one could condemn him.

The word "reckoned" or "credited" comes from the banking realm. It refers to money placed in a person's account, either by that person himself or by someone else on his behalf.

—◦ *What sort of people does God justify? What encouragement do you take from this truth?* (Romans 4:5)

—◦ *What is the one condition for justification in the eyes of God?* (Romans 5:1)

—◦ *Why can we never be justified (declared righteous by God) on the basis of rule-keeping or by obeying the law?* (Romans 3:20)

—⟨ *How can the death of Christ be the ground of our justification?* (*Romans* 3:24–25)

—⟨ *Can any of us boast that our good works (keeping the laws, obeying the rules) played a part in our justification? Why or why not?* (*Romans* 3:27–28)

—⟨ *Was Abraham justified by his works or by his faith?* (*Genesis* 15:6; *Romans* 4:1–2)

—⟨ *Your friend Andy has been thinking about his own spiritual journey and truly wants to know Christ personally. But he struggles with deep guilt over his sinful past. When you tell him that God will accept him by faith alone (and not by good works), he has a hard time believing you. He thinks he needs to "clean up his act" before he comes to Christ. On the basis of the verses in this section, how will you answer him? Note especially Romans 4:5. What truth does Andy need to know?*

PART THREE

OUR SIN AND CHRIST'S DEATH

People have many ways of trying to deal with the problem of sin. Most of them involve doing something in order to be right with God, gain His favor, win forgiveness, and earn a place in heaven.

Name some religious things that people might do in order to win forgiveness and earn a place in heaven.

Name some good deeds that people might do for the same purpose.

—◦ *Can being religious or doing good deeds help you win forgiveness or earn a place in heaven? Why or why not? See Galatians* 2:16 *and Titus* 3:5.

—◦ *How good do you have to be to go to heaven?*

❏ Pretty good

❏ Really good

❏ Better than my next-door neighbor

❏ Perfect

(Hint: If you answer anything other than "D", go back and review Session Two.)

In Session One we saw that, although there is nothing we can do to bridge the gap between us and God, Christ has made a way for our sins to be forgiven. The cross is the "bridge" that takes us to heaven. This is what the Bible means when it says that Jesus is the "way" to the Father (John 14:6).

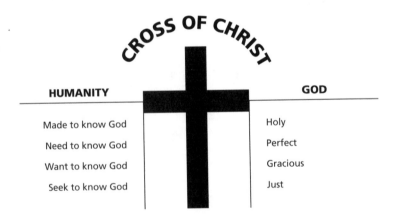

- Why is the cross of Christ the only way to bridge the gap between God and man?

• If we don't want to come to God by way of the cross, is He obligated to provide some other way for us to go to heaven? Why or why not?

PART FOUR ◦
SWAPPING GRADES WITH JESUS

Let's suppose that God keeps "grades" in the "principal's office" in heaven. Since God demands perfection, even one failure in any "course" means you flunk that course entirely. The news about your grades isn't good. Let's look at your grades and compare them to Jesus who finished at the "head of the class."

YOU	JESUS
Seeking God – F	Seeking God – A
Doing Good – F	Doing Good – A
Obeying God – F	Obeying God – A
Keeping the Law – F	Keeping the Law – A
Being Perfect – F	Being Perfect – A

—◦ *Do your "grades" seem fair to you? Why or why not?*

—◦ *Do you agree with the "grades" Jesus earned? (Hebrews 4:15)*

—◦ *Would you like to "swap grades" with Jesus? According to 2 Corinthians 5:21, how is that possible?*

God has a simple proposition for you. If you admit you are a sinner, He offers to declare you righteous. All you have to do is come to Jesus. Trust in Him, and your sins will be forgiven, your record in heaven will be wiped clean, and you will be declared righteous in the eyes of God.

❑ I believe this is true.

❑ This doesn't make sense to me.

❑ I need to think about this for a while.

A VERSE TO MEMORIZE

*"And to the one who does not
work but trusts him who justifies
the ungodly, his faith is counted
as righteousness."*

Romans 4:5 ESV

A PRAYER FOR THOSE IN NEED OF SALVATION

*My Lord and my God, Your Word tells me that I am a sinner through and through, that I
was born a sinner, that I am a sinner, and that sin will stay with me until the day I die. It
tells me that apart from Your grace I am lost, hopeless, defiled, blind, and spiritually dead. If
this is true, my only hope is in You. If I am ever to be saved, it must be only by Your grace.
You sent Jesus to be a mediator, to pay the price, to turn away Your wrath so that the door
to heaven might be opened. I stand at the door, hoping to be admitted to Your presence. Show
me what You require that I might spend eternity with You. Amen.*

A Truth to Remember

GOD IS OFFERING YOU
SALVATION FREE OF CHARGE.
JESUS PAID IN FULL SO
YOU WOULDN'T HAVE
TO PAY ANYTHING.

ADDITIONAL RESOURCES

John H. Armstrong, ed., *This We Believe*, Zondervan Publishing House, 2000.

Billy Graham, *Peace With God: The Secret of Happiness*, Word Publishing, 2000.

John Blanchard, *Right With God*, Banner of Truth, 1996.

Phil Newton, *The Way of Faith*, Founders Press, 2002.

R. C. Sproul, *Essential Truths of the Christian Faith*, Tyndale House Publishers, 1998.

—⊛ SESSION SEVEN ⊛—

What is Saving Faith?

PART ONE ⊛—
WALKING THE TIGHTROPE

In the 19th century the greatest tightrope walker in the world was a man named Charles Blondin. On June 30, 1859, he became the first man in history to walk on a tightrope across Niagara Falls. Over 25,000 people gathered to watch him walk 1,100 feet suspended on a tiny rope 160 feet above the raging waters. He worked without a net or safety harness of any kind. The slightest slip would prove fatal. When he safely reached the Canadian side, the crowd burst into a mighty roar.

In the days that followed he would walk across the Falls many times. Once he walked across on stilts, another time he took a chair and a stove with him and sat down midway across, cooked an omelet and ate it. Once he carried his manager across riding piggyback. And once he pushed a wheelbarrow across loaded with 350 pounds of cement. On one occasion he asked the cheering spectators if they thought he could push a man across sitting in a wheelbarrow. A mighty roar of approval rose from the crowd. Spying a man cheering loudly, he asked, "Sir, do you think I could safely carry you across in this wheelbarrow?" "Yes, of course." "Get in," the Great Blondin replied with a smile. The man refused.

That makes it clear, doesn't it? It's one thing to believe a man can walk across by himself. It's another thing to believe he could safely carry you across. How much faith does it take to go to heaven? It depends. The answer is not much and all you've got. If you are willing to trust Jesus Christ with as much faith as you happen to have, you can be saved. But if you're holding anything back, thinking that maybe you need to do something to help save yourself, forget it! True saving faith expresses itself by reaching out to take Christ as our Savior and Lord—and not before then.

- It may be expressed through a prayer of personal trust in Christ.
- It may be expressed through baptism.
- It may be expressed through a "public profession."

But those things alone are not saving faith. Saving faith understands the gospel, believes the gospel, and then commits to the gospel as the only hope of salvation. Saving faith reaches out and trusts Christ as Lord and Savior.

—⌐ *List some religious activities that people may use as a substitute for true saving faith.*

—⌐ *Name some reasons people give for not coming to Christ for salvation.*

—⌐ *According to Hebrews 11:6, what is the one thing necessary in order for us to please God?*

Which, if any, of the following activities proves that you have true saving faith?

❑ Being raised in the church

❑ Being baptized

❑ Giving money to the church

❑ Serving as a Sunday school teacher

❑ Taking communion

❑ Praying every day

❑ Speaking in tongues

❑ Saying the "Our Father"

❑ Walking forward during an invitation

❑ Signing a "Decision Card"

❑ Obeying the Ten Commandments

PART TWO
KNOWLEDGE, CONVICTION, COMMITMENT

True saving faith involves the intellect, the emotions, and the will. The faith that saves us involves all that we are in coming to Christ. Faith starts with knowledge, moves to conviction, and ends with commitment.

🅐 Knowledge

1. Why is knowledge the first step in true faith?

2. Name some things we must understand before we can truly believe in Christ.

🅑 Conviction

1. Why is faith more than simply knowing the facts about Jesus?

2. Read Matthew 8:5–13. Why did Jesus marvel at the centurion's faith? How do we know that his faith went beyond knowledge?

🅒 Commitment

1. Why is commitment a necessary part of true saving faith?

2. Read John 20:26–29. When Thomas finally met Jesus after the resurrection, how did he express his total commitment to Christ?

Let's personalize John 3:16 (ESV). Insert your name in the blanks in this verse. "For God so loved _____, that he gave his only Son, that whoever (_____) believes in him should not perish but have eternal life." Describe the level of your faith in Jesus Christ at this moment. Is it mostly knowledge without much conviction? Is it conviction without commitment? Or it is knowledge plus conviction plus commitment? If you aren't sure, just say, "I'm not sure" or "I'm still thinking about it."

PART THREE ✐
WHAT ABOUT REPENTANCE?

The very first word Jesus spoke in his public ministry was the word "repent." The word repentance literally means "to change the mind." It has to do with the way you think about something. You've been thinking one way, but now you think differently. That's repentance—the changing of the mind. Repentance is a change in the way you think that leads to change in the way you live. When you really change your mind about something, it's going to change the way you think about it, talk about it, feel about it, and ultimately what you do about it.

1 According to Isaiah 59:20, what must we repent of?

2 What is the result of repentance? (Luke 3:3)

3 What happens to those who do not repent? (Luke 13:1–5)

4 1 Thessalonians 1:9–10 offers a good picture of how repentance works:

Step 1: You turned to _____ from _____ (verse 9).

Step 2: You now _____ the living and true God (verse 9).

Step 3: You are _____ for Jesus to return from heaven (verse 10)

5 According to 2 Peter 3:9, what does God want everyone to do?

6 What is the evidence of true repentance? (Matthew 3:8; Acts 26:20)

7 Based on these verses, write your own definition of repentance.

8 Why is true repentance necessary for salvation?

EPENTANCE AND FAITH

rue repentance and saving faith go together. They are like two sides of the same oin. To repent means to change my mind about whatever is keeping me from coming to Christ. To trust Christ means to wholeheartedly reach out to Him by faith so at He becomes my Savior and Lord.

or each of the following statements, write "Agree" or "Do not agree" or "Not sure."

_____ As long as I believe in Jesus, I know I'm going to heaven.

_____ If you say you believe in Jesus, you can sin as much as you want and still be saved.

_____ If you don't accept Christ as Savior, you can't go to heaven.

_____ Faith is a crutch for those who need it.

_____ Faith means wholehearted trust in Jesus Christ and Him alone.

_____ It takes more faith *not* to believe in Jesus than to believe in Him.

_____ If you have faith in God but not in Jesus, you'll still go to heaven.

_____ If you believe in Jesus, you don't need to go to church.

_____ Faith plus good works—that's the key to salvation!

_____ True faith is a gift from God.

_____ The more you know, the more faith you're bound to have.

✛ ✛

PART FOUR ⌒
THE POWER OF FEEBLE FAITH

Many people wonder if they have "enough" faith to believe. Luke 8:40–48 tells of a woman with very little faith who received a great miracle from the Lord.

—◦ *How long had this woman been sick? Before she met Jesus, what was her prognosis?* (verse 43)

—◦ *Why do you suppose she touched His garment from behind?* (verse 44)

—◦ *Have you felt like you were in a hopeless situation? If you prayed about it, what did you ask God to do? How were your prayers answered?*

—◦ *Although Jesus was surrounded by many people, He felt this woman's feeble touch* (verse 45). *Why did He single out this woman for special attention?*

—◦ *How did the woman respond to Jesus?* (verse 47)

—◦ *The word "healed" in verse 48 can also mean "saved" or "delivered." What was the basis for her healing?*

—◦ *Has God done something wonderful for you recently? Have you told anyone else about it?*

How simple it is to come to Christ. Only a touch and this woman was healed. Not by her toiling, not by her promises to do better, not by an offer to do something for Jesus if He would do something for her. No deals here. She reached out a trembling hand and, in an instant, she was healed. It wasn't even a long process. It happened so fast that it could only be called a miracle.

SOME PERSONAL QUESTIONS: What, if anything, holds you back from making a full commitment of your life to Jesus Christ right now? Are there issues that stand in the way? What would it take for you to say "yes" to Jesus as Savior and Lord?

A VERSE TO MEMORIZE

"Behold, I stand at the door and knock. If anyone hears my voice and opens the door, I will come in to him and eat with him, and he with me."
Revelation 3:20 ESV

A PRAYER FOR TRUE FAITH

O Lord, when I read Your Word, there are many things I do not understand. And the more I learn, the more I realize how far I have to go in my spiritual journey. Help me to truly believe the things I do understand. May my doubts never stand in the way of my faith. I seek full assurance of the truth so that I may know with certainty that my sins are forgiven and that I have eternal life. May my knowledge lead to conviction and my conviction to commitment. Lord, I want to believe. Help me. Amen.

A Truth to Remember

SAVING FAITH UNDERSTANDS
THE GOSPEL, BELIEVES
THE GOSPEL, AND THEN
COMMITS TO THE GOSPEL
AS THE ONLY HOPE OF
SALVATION. SAVING FAITH
REACHES OUT AND TRUSTS
CHRIST AS LORD AND SAVIOR.

ADDITIONAL RESOURCES

Tony Evans, *Totally Saved*, Moody Press, 2002.

R. Kent Hughes, *Sought by Grace*, Moody Press, 2002.

Ray Pritchard, *Faith*, Moody Press, 2001.

Charles Ryrie, *So Great Salvation*, Moody Press, 1997.

Lee Strobel, *The Case for Faith*, Zondervan Publishing House, 2000.

~ SESSION EIGHT ~
Coming to Christ

PART ONE ~
A RELATIONSHIP, NOT JUST RELIGION

Here's an e-mail telling about a question asked by a co-worker:

> How is a Christian defined? It used to be that if you were not Jewish or Hindu or Buddhist, you were a Christian, whether Catholic or Lutheran or Episcopal or Baptist. But it seems now that the word means something more specific. Is it considered to be an actual religion other than Catholic or Lutheran or Episcopal or Baptist or whatever? If so, what makes it different?

That's a very good question. This writer has penetrated to a core issue that has long confused millions of people: *What is the difference between being a Christian and being a church member?* The simplest way to answer that question is to say that a Christian is a person who has come to know God deeply and personally through genuine saving faith in the Lord Jesus Christ. To say it that way means that, while nearly all Christians are church members, not all church members are necessarily true Christians. Knowing God through Christ is about a personal relationship made possible through faith; it is not about religious ritual or merely "joining a church."

That truth leads us to an important point: No one "drifts" into Christianity by accident. At some point you must consciously trust Christ as Lord and Savior. In the words of Charles Spurgeon, "You will never go to heaven in a crowd." It's true there will be crowds in heaven, but we only go there one at a time. God saves individuals, not masses or groups.

There comes a time when you must decide where you stand with Jesus. No one can sit on the fence forever. Not to decide is a decision in itself. If you don't say yes to Christ, you are actually saying no. There is an "hour of decision" that comes to all of us sooner or later. In this final session of our study, you will have an opportunity to make a personal decision to come to Christ as Lord and Savior.

—❧ *Why do so many people confuse being a Christian with being a member of a Christian church? What's the essential difference between a real Christian and a religious person?*

—❧ *Why is it necessary to make a personal decision to follow Christ? Have you ever made that choice for yourself?*

—❧ *Read John 3:1–7. Jesus said to Nicodemus, "You must be _____ again." What does that statement mean?*

If the cross is the "bridge" that takes us to heaven, then each one of us has a decision to make. A bridge will do us no good unless we walk across it to the other side. Even so, the death of Christ will not change us until we trust Christ as Savior. Which side of the bridge are you on right now? Circle the answer below that represents your current location.

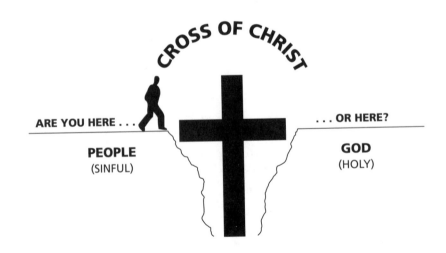

CROSS OF CHRIST

ARE YOU HERE . . .   . . . OR HERE?

PEOPLE
(SINFUL)

GOD
(HOLY)

PART TWO
SALVATION MADE SIMPLE

"Yet to all who received him, to those who believed in his name, he gave the right to become children of God—children born not of natural descent, nor of human decision or a husband's will, but born of God" (John 1:12–13). This passage offers a simple outline of what it means to come to Christ for salvation. These questions will help focus our thinking on this vital topic.

—◦ *What does it mean to "receive" Christ?*

—◦ *All are created by God, but not everyone in the world is a child of God. Sometimes people carelessly say, "We're all God's children," but the Bible says no such thing. God only gives the privilege of being His children to those who by personal faith receive Jesus as Lord and Savior. Do you agree or disagree?*

—◦ *True or false: If my parents were Christians, then I am automatically a Christian too.*

—◦ *Why is receiving Christ also called being "born of God"? What important truth does that tell us about the ultimate source of salvation?*

—◦ *Have you received Christ as your Lord and Savior? What is the basis for your answer?*

PUT THE WORD IN YOUR HEART

Before going on, take time to read John 1:12–13 out loud. In order to make this powerful passage a part of your life, why not take time to memorize it? Read the passage out loud daily. Write it on a card and carry the card with you so you can review the verses wherever you go. Allow John's message about Jesus to change your life forever!

PART THREE ∂—
THE BLESSINGS OF SALVATION

The New Testament lists many blessings and privileges that come to us the moment we trust Christ as Savior. Check out these verses to see what they promise to those who believe in Jesus. Write your answer beside each verse.

1 Peter 1:20 _____

Galatians 3:26 _____

Romans 5:1 _____

Ephesians 1:7 _____

Ephesians 1:13–14 _____

Galatians 2:20 _____

Galatians 4:7 _____

John 6:47 _____

Romans 8:38–39 _____

PART FOUR ∂—
A PRAYER THAT COULD CHANGE YOUR LIFE

Let's review what we've learned in this Bible study series. Listed below are a number of summary statements. Put a check mark by each statement if you agree with it.

❑ God is infinite, eternal, holy, righteous, all-knowing, all-powerful. He created me in His image.

❑ God loves me and wants to have a relationship with me.

❑ I was made to know God personally.

❑ I am a sinner.

❑ My sins separate me from God.

❑ I am truly guilty and unable to save myself.

❑ I can never be good enough to save myself.

❑ God sent His Son, Jesus Christ, to be my Savior.

❑ Jesus died on the cross for my sins.

❑ Jesus rose from the dead on the third day.

❑ I am not saved by what I do but by what Christ has done for me.

❑ When I trust Christ, He takes my sin and I receive the gift of His righteousness.

❑ Salvation is a free gift offered to anyone who trusts Christ as Savior.

❑ I am ready to receive Christ as my Lord and my Savior.

Perhaps it will help you to form your words into a very simple prayer. Even though I encourage you to pray this prayer, I caution you that saying words alone will not save you. Prayer doesn't save. Only Christ can save. But prayer can be a means of reaching out to the Lord in true saving faith. If you pray these words in faith, Christ will save you. You can be sure of that.

Lord Jesus, for too long I've kept You out of my life. I know that I am a sinner and that I cannot save myself. No longer will I close the door when I hear You knocking. By faith I gratefully receive Your gift of salvation. I am ready to trust You as my Lord and Savior. Thank You, Lord Jesus, for coming to Earth. I believe You are the Son of God who died on the cross for my sins and rose from the dead on the third day. Thank You for bearing my sins and giving me the gift of eternal life. I believe Your words are true. Come into my heart, Lord Jesus, and be my Savior. Amen.

Signed _____ Date _____

In the end I can't believe for you, or you for me. Jesus said, "Come unto me." Will you come? Come and see for yourself. Come and discover how Christ can change your life.

If you are fearful, put your heart at ease. He avoids no seeker. He will not turn you away. You will see for yourself. God invites you. But still you must come. Do not hesitate. Stop making excuses. Come to Christ and be saved. Trust in Him, and your new life will begin.

NOW THAT YOU BELIEVE . . .

Trusting Christ as Savior and Lord is the most important decision you will ever make. Your eternal destiny has been changed because of what Christ has done for you. But that is not the end of the story. In many ways, it is only the beginning. You will soon discover that, when Christ comes into your life, He changes it from the inside out. As He makes Himself at home in your heart, you will discover new desires you never had before and new strength to empower your new desires. The Christian life begins the moment you trust Christ, but it doesn't end there. It continues day by day as you learn to walk with God, to grow in faith and love, to pray to your Heavenly Father, to follow Jesus wherever He leads you, and to share His love with those you meet. If the Christian life is a book, coming to Christ is only chapter 1.

—*What are the next steps you need to take on your spiritual journey?*

—*If you have just trusted Christ as Savior, who else needs to know about your decision?*

Becoming a Christian means taking a journey that starts on Earth and ends in heaven. If you have gotten this far in the Anchor Bible study, I believe you are well on your way in your journey with the Lord. Keep moving forward, keep your eyes on the prize, and you will not be disappointed. In the spiritual life, direction makes all the difference. God is more interested in direction than perfection. Now that you have committed your life to Christ, there will be many surprises, some wonderful answers to prayer, and no doubt some major battles to fight. You may find yourself going up and down in your Christian life. If that happens, don't despair. Just keep moving forward with Christ. Daily obedience is the key. The Holy Spirit will help you to obey the Lord.

A Seven-Day Plan for Spiritual Growth

Day 1	Read John 3. Circle every instance of the word "believe" or "believes".
Day 2	Tell a friend about your decision to trust Christ as Savior.
Day 3	Spend time today praying for spiritual guidance.
Day 4	Memorize Philippians 4:13. Share it with a friend.
Day 5	Ask God to lead you to someone who needs a word of encouragement.
Day 6	Meditate on Psalm 1. Write it down word for word and then say it out loud.
Day 7	Find a church where the Bible is taught. Attend worship services this Sunday.

A VERSE TO MEMORIZE

"I write these things to you who believe in the name of the Son of God that you may know that you have eternal life."

1 John 5:13 ESV

A PRAYER FOR SPIRITUAL GROWTH

Lord, now that I believe with all my heart, I want to grow each day as a Christian. Thank You for forgiving all my sins. I praise You for the gift of salvation and the honor of being Your child and a member of Your family. If I should die tonight, I know that I will wake up in heaven. While I am on the Earth, may I grow in love for You and in love for those around me. Help me to live so that others see Jesus in me. I ask this in my Savior's name. Amen.

A Truth to Remember

COMING TO CHRIST BY FAITH
IS A LIFETIME JOURNEY THAT
STARTS ON EARTH AND ENDS
IN HEAVEN.

ADDITIONAL RESOURCES

Oswald Chambers, *My Utmost for His Highest*, Discovery House Publishers, 1992.

Erwin Lutzer, *How You Can Be Sure You Will Spend Eternity With God*, Moody Press, 1996.

Ray Pritchard, *FAQ: Frequently Asked Questions About the Christian Life*, Broadman & Holman, 2001.

Ray Pritchard, *What a Christian Believes*, Crossway Books, 1998.

Colin Smith, *Unlocking the Bible Story, Volumes 1–4*, Moody Press, 2002.

William L. Thrasher, *Basics for Believers, Volume 1*, Moody Press, 1998.

William L. Thrasher, *Basics for Believers, Volume 2*, Moody Press, 2000.